LONG HARE STUDIOS
MONSTERS, MAGIC & MYTH
ADULT COLORING BOOK

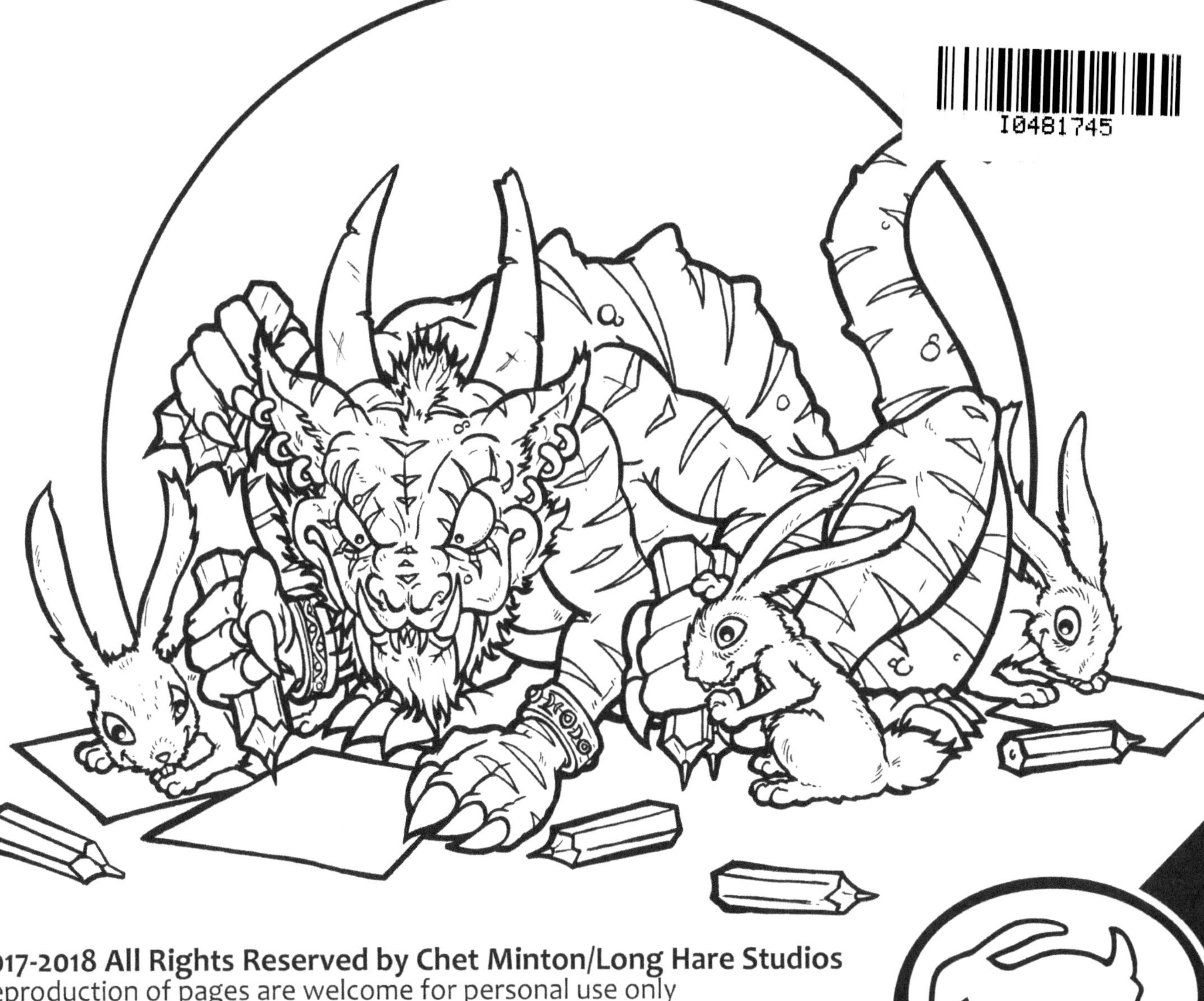

I0481745

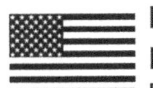
ISBN Number-13: 978-1981528042
ISBN Number-10: 1981528040
Printed by Amazon/CreateSpace

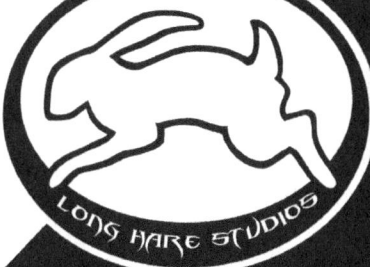

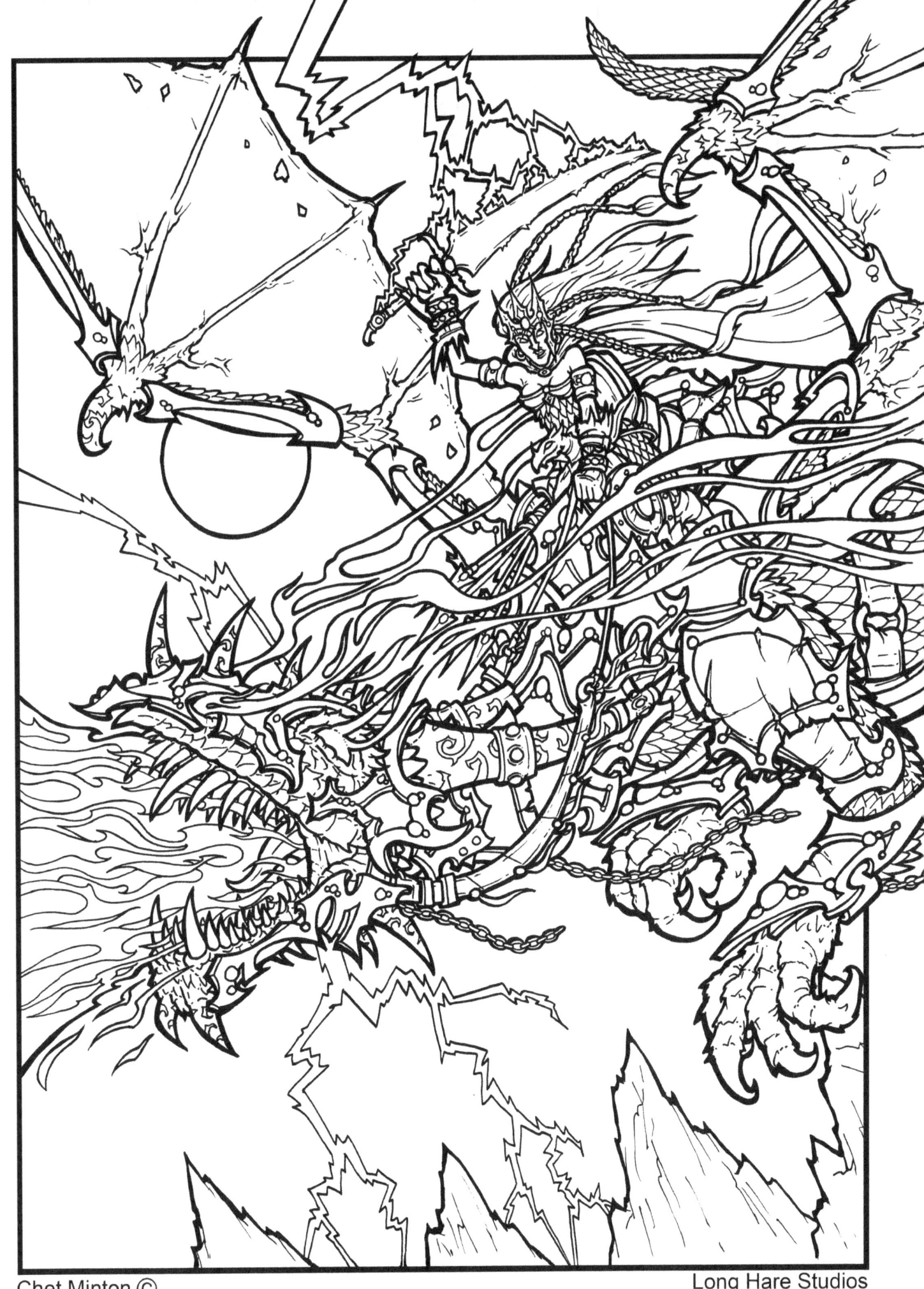

Chet Minton ©

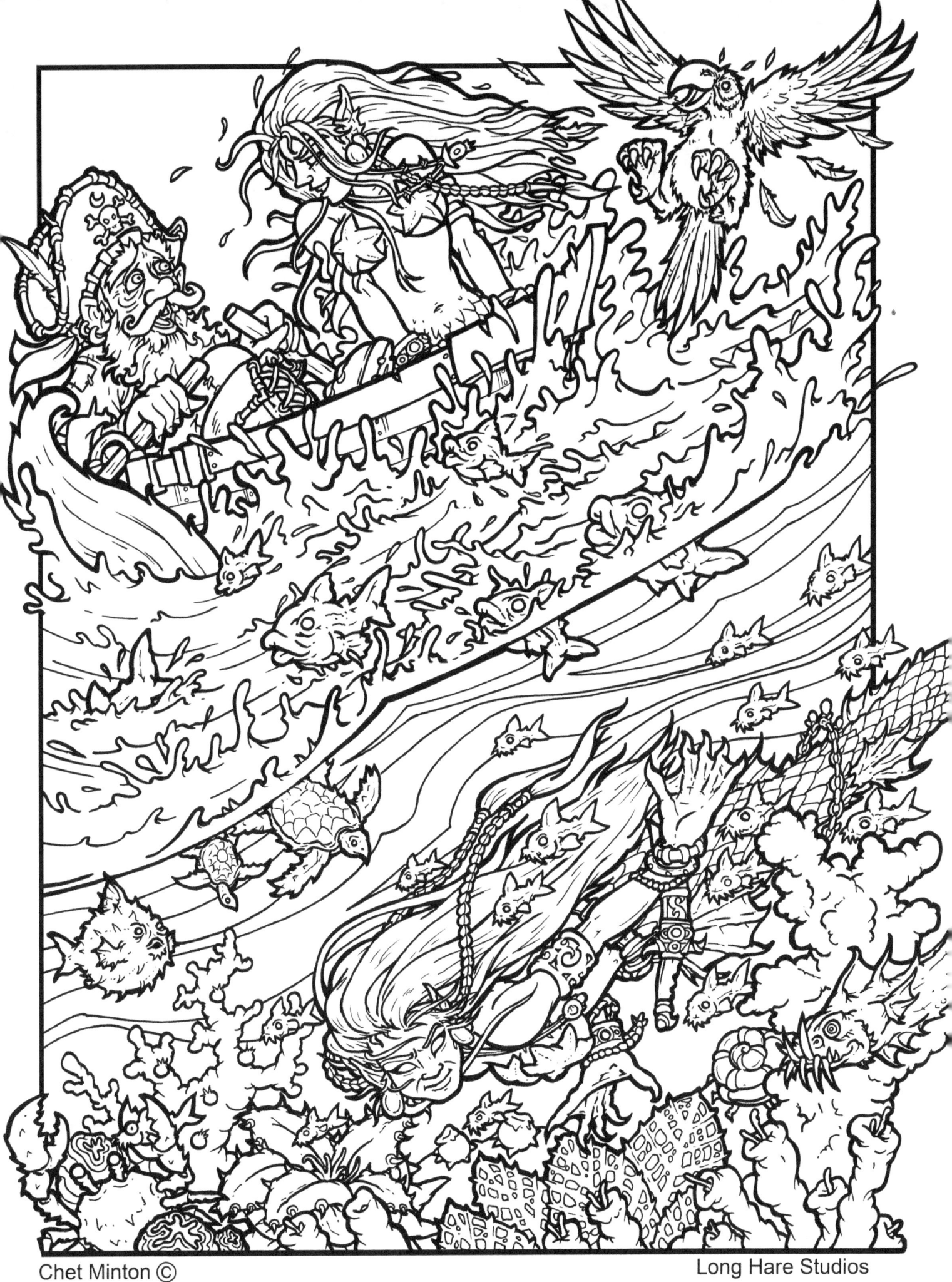

Chet Minton ©

Long Hare Studios

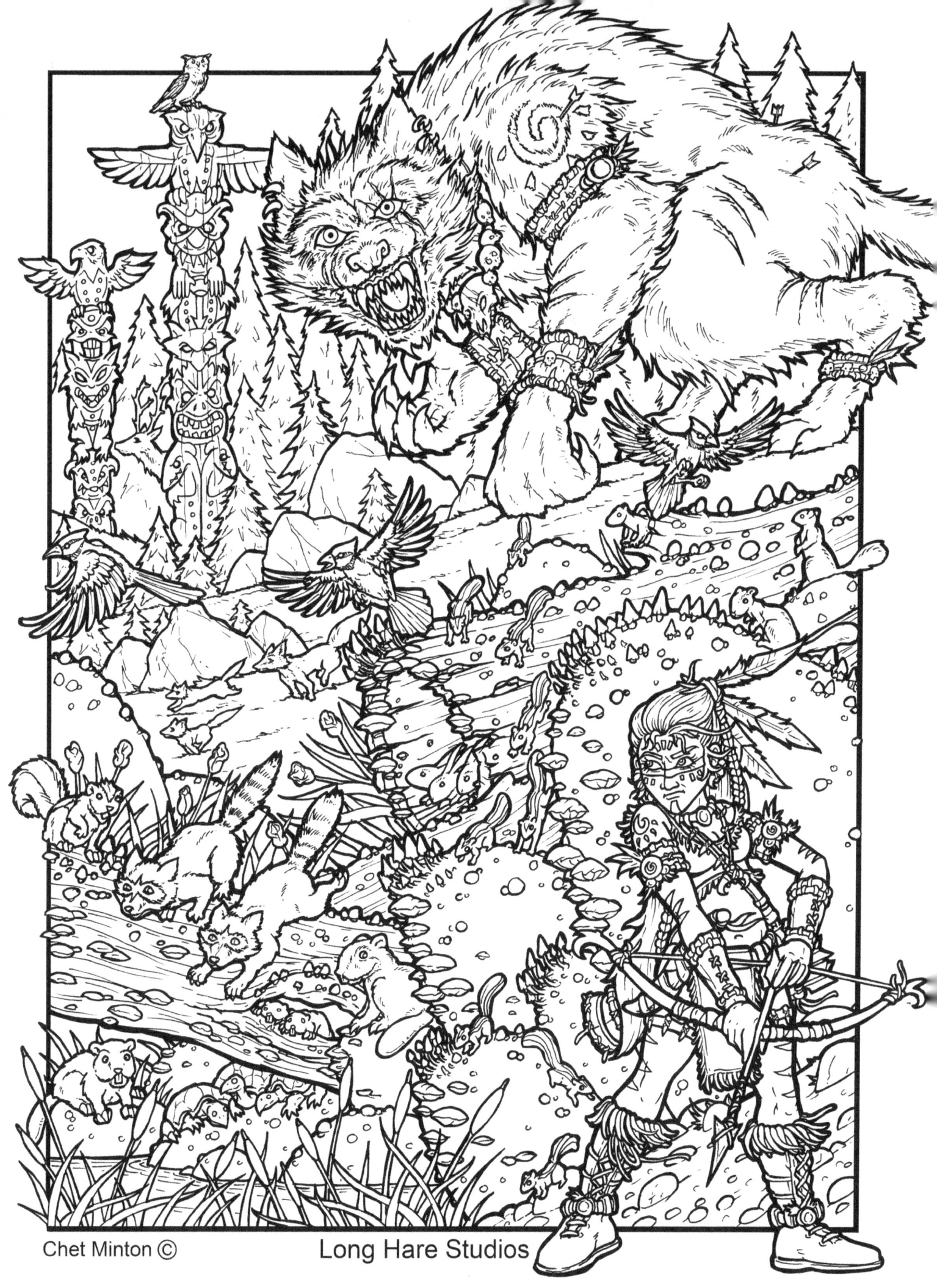

Long Hare Studios

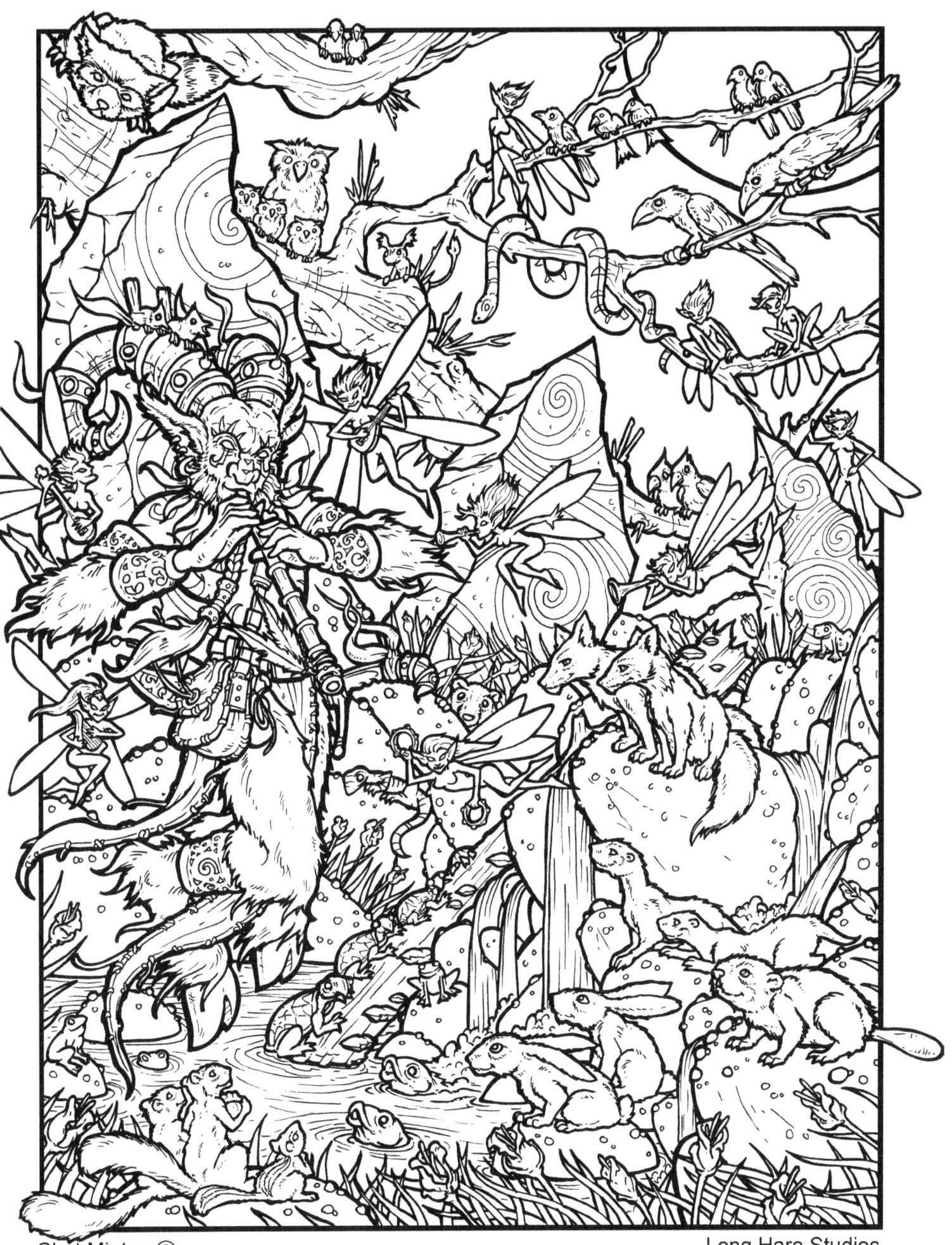

Chet Minton ©

Long Hare Studios

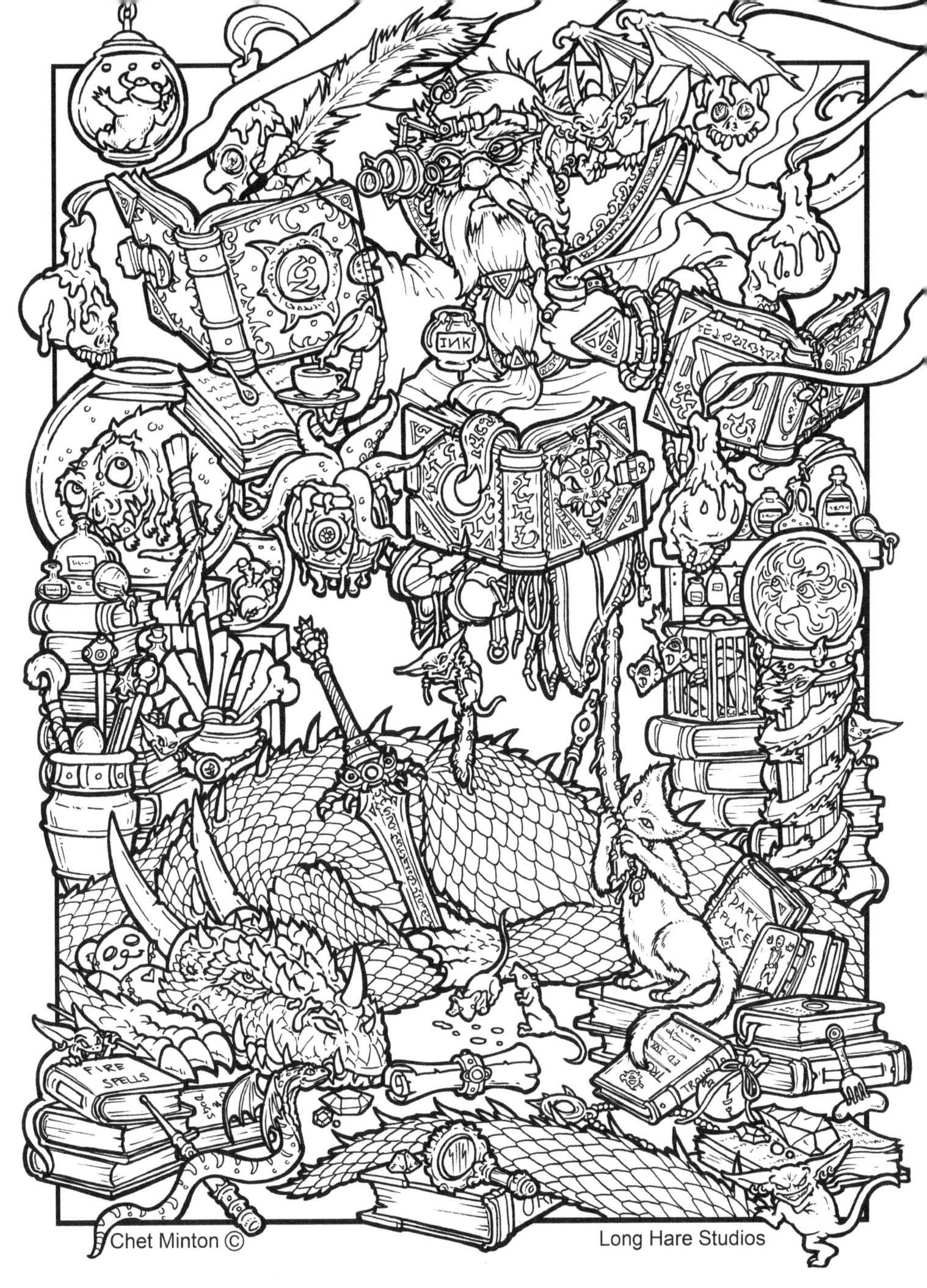

Chet Minton ©

Long Hare Studios

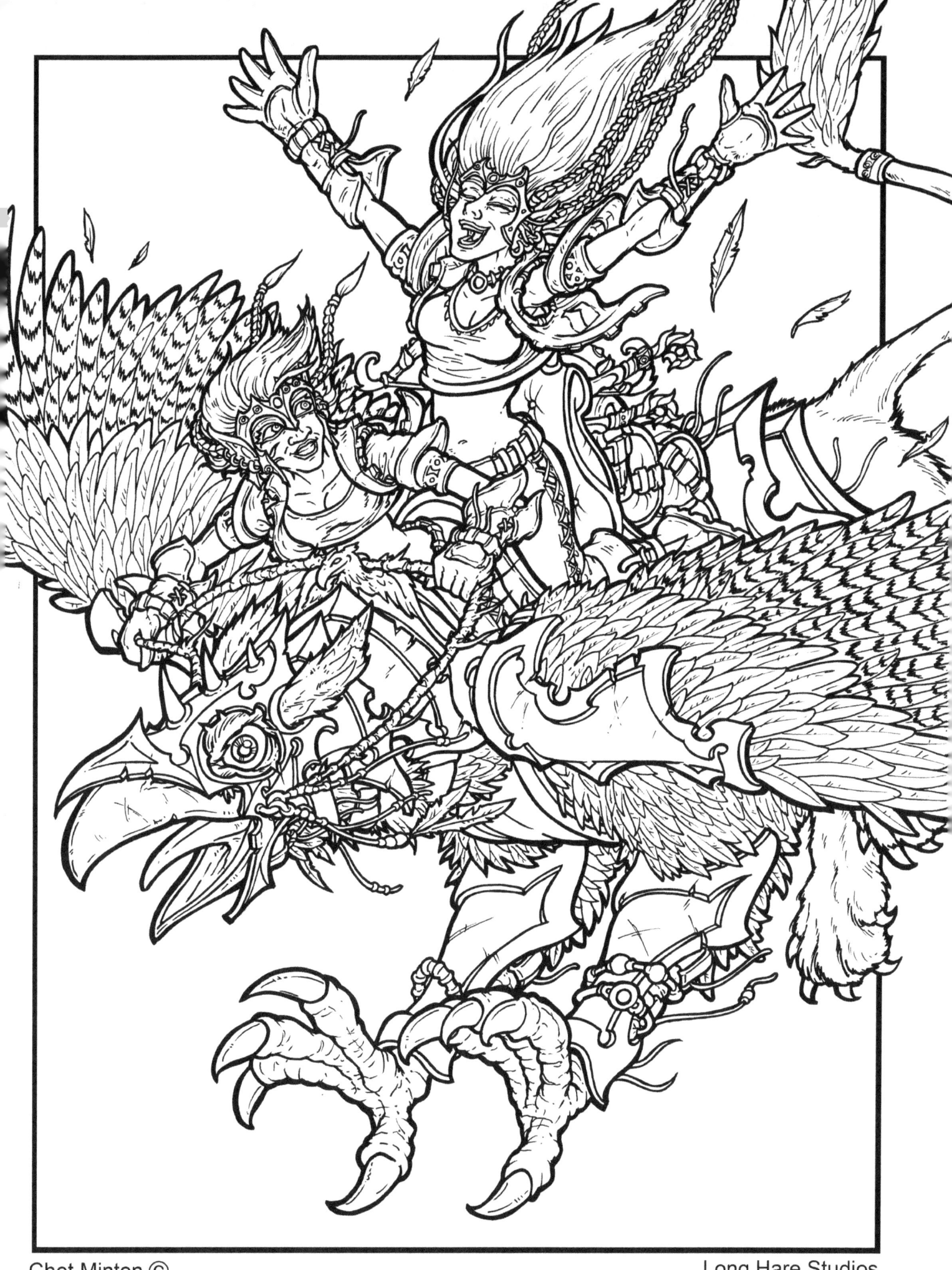

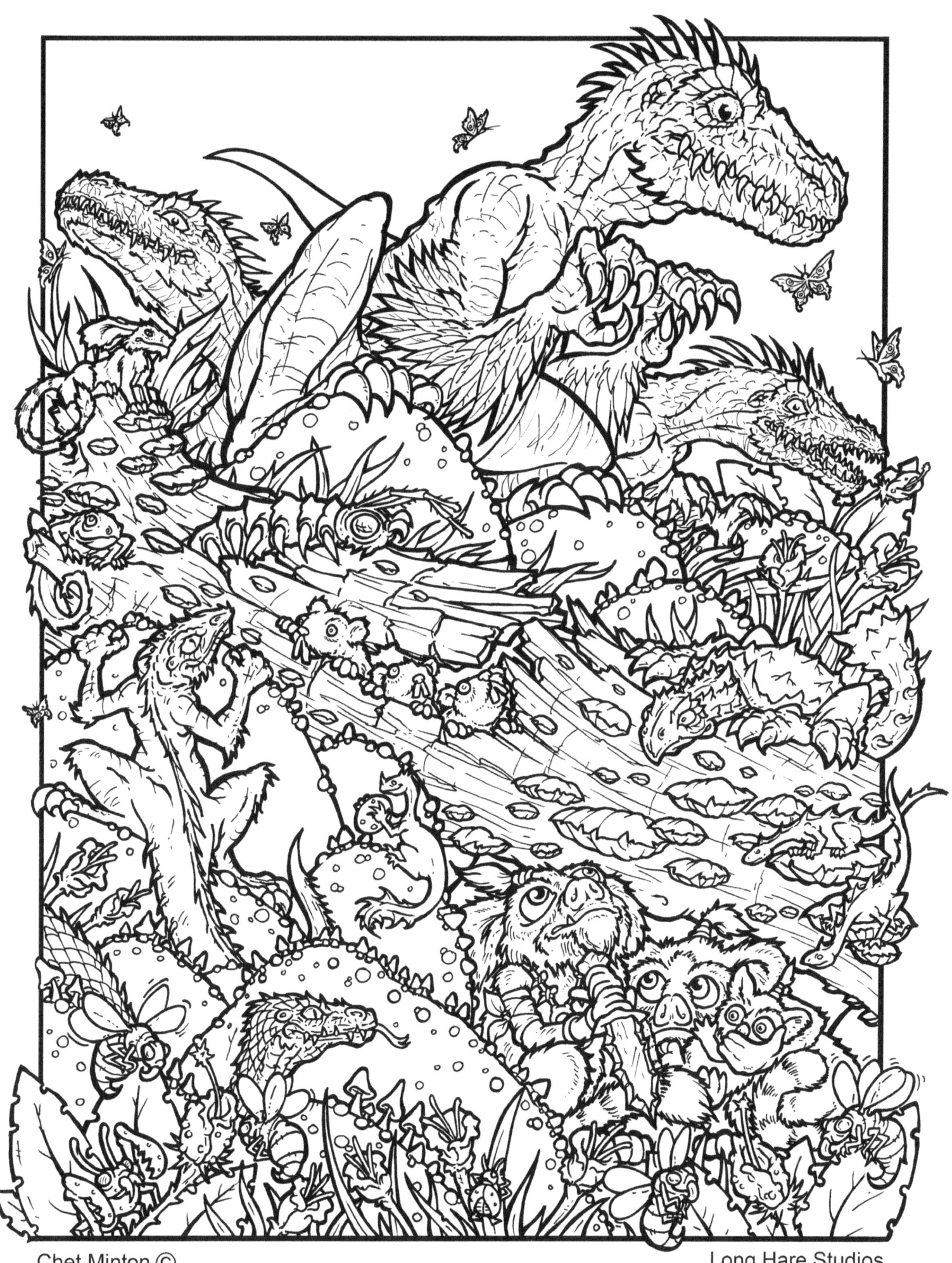

Chet Minton ©

Long Hare Studios

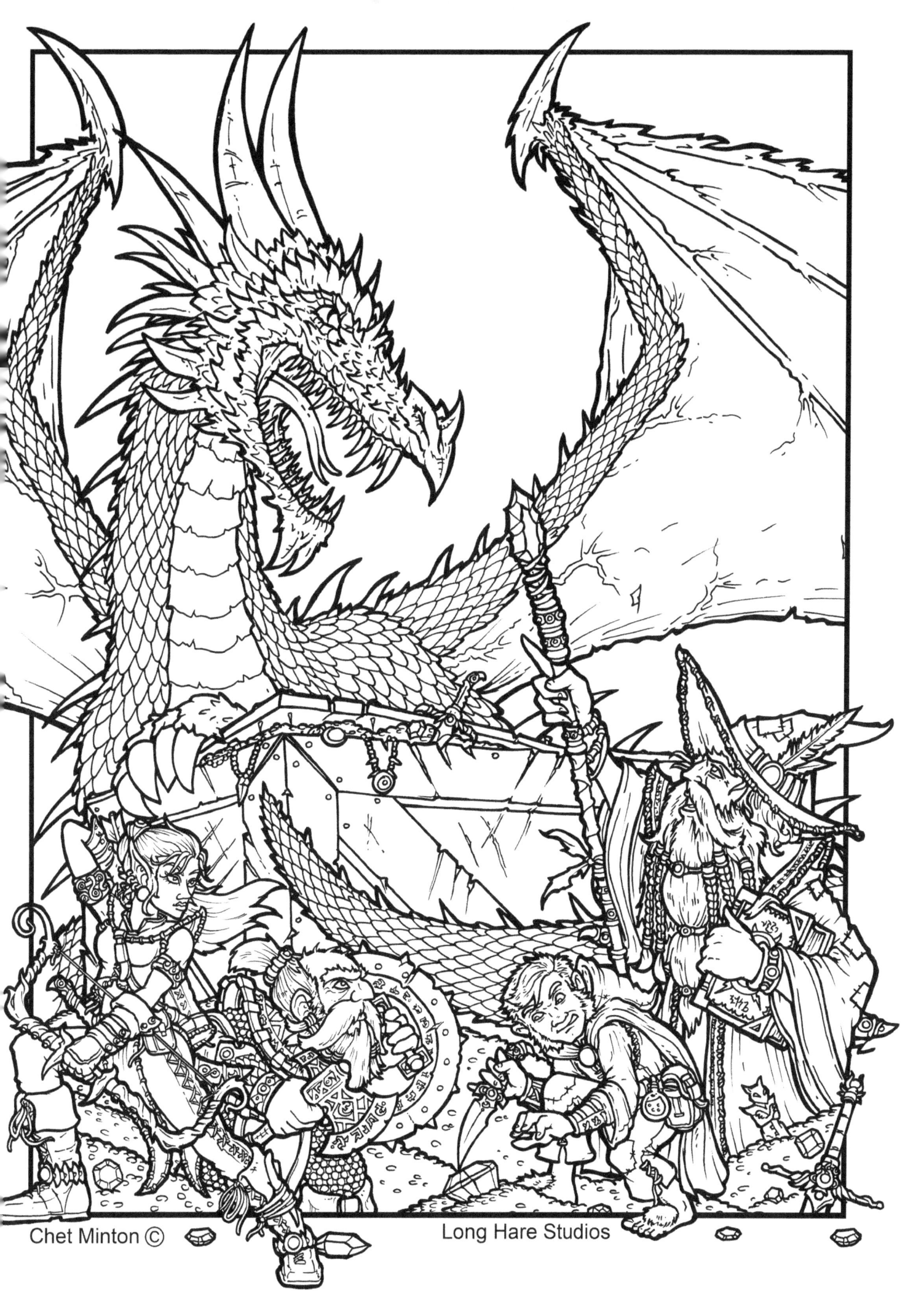

Chet Minton ©   Long Hare Studios

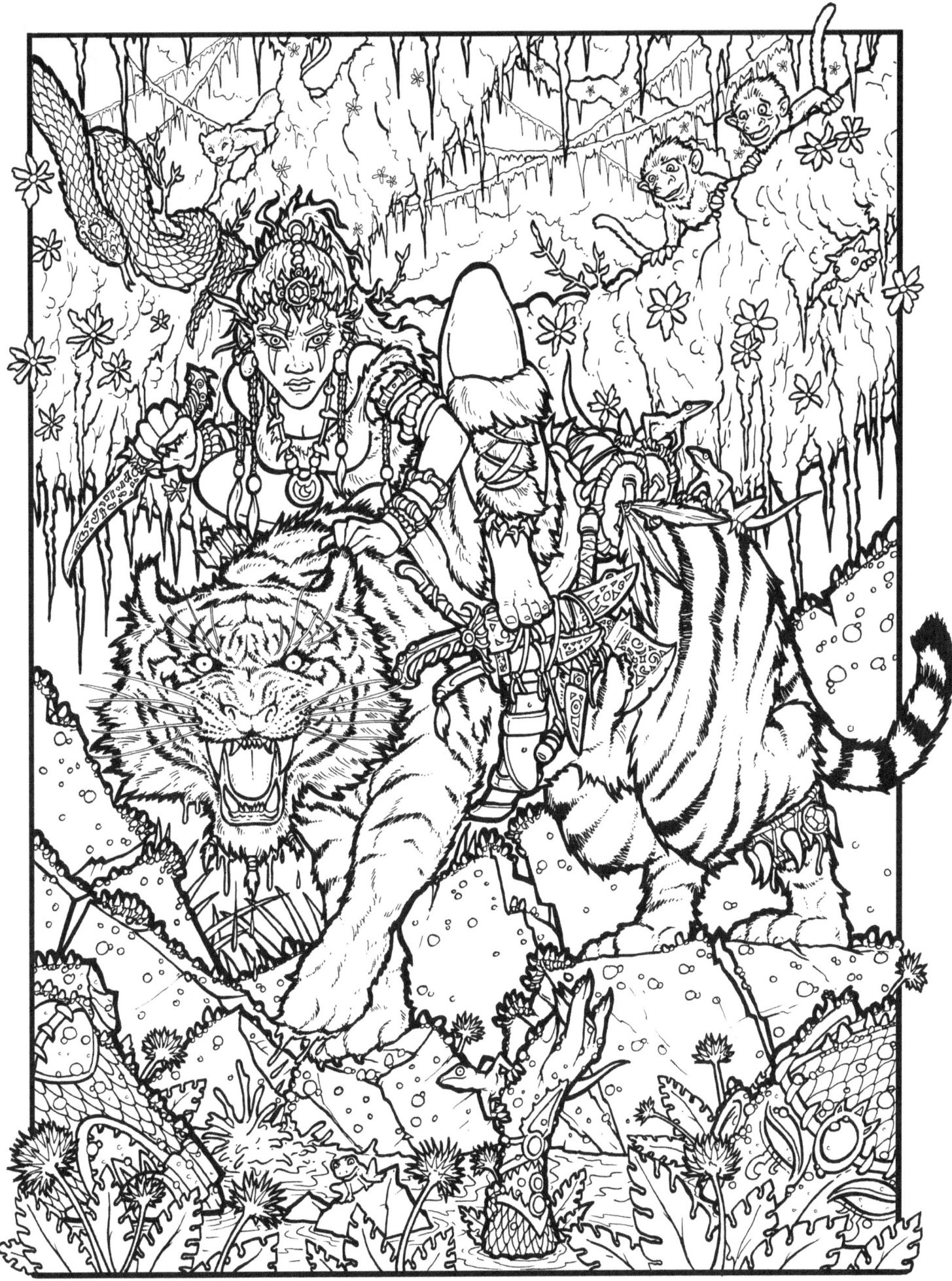

Chet Minton ©

Long Hare Studios

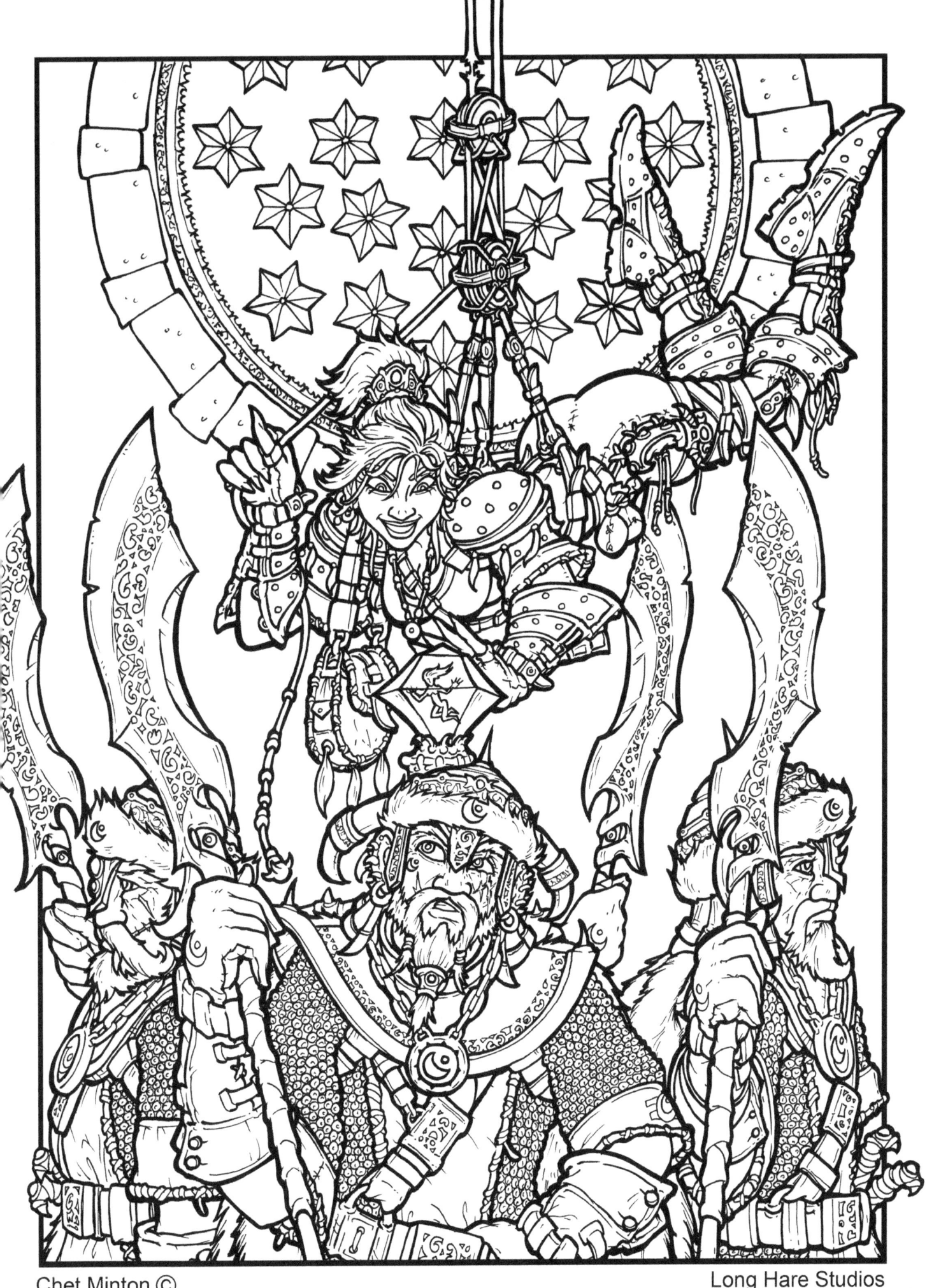

Chet Minton ©

Long Hare Studios

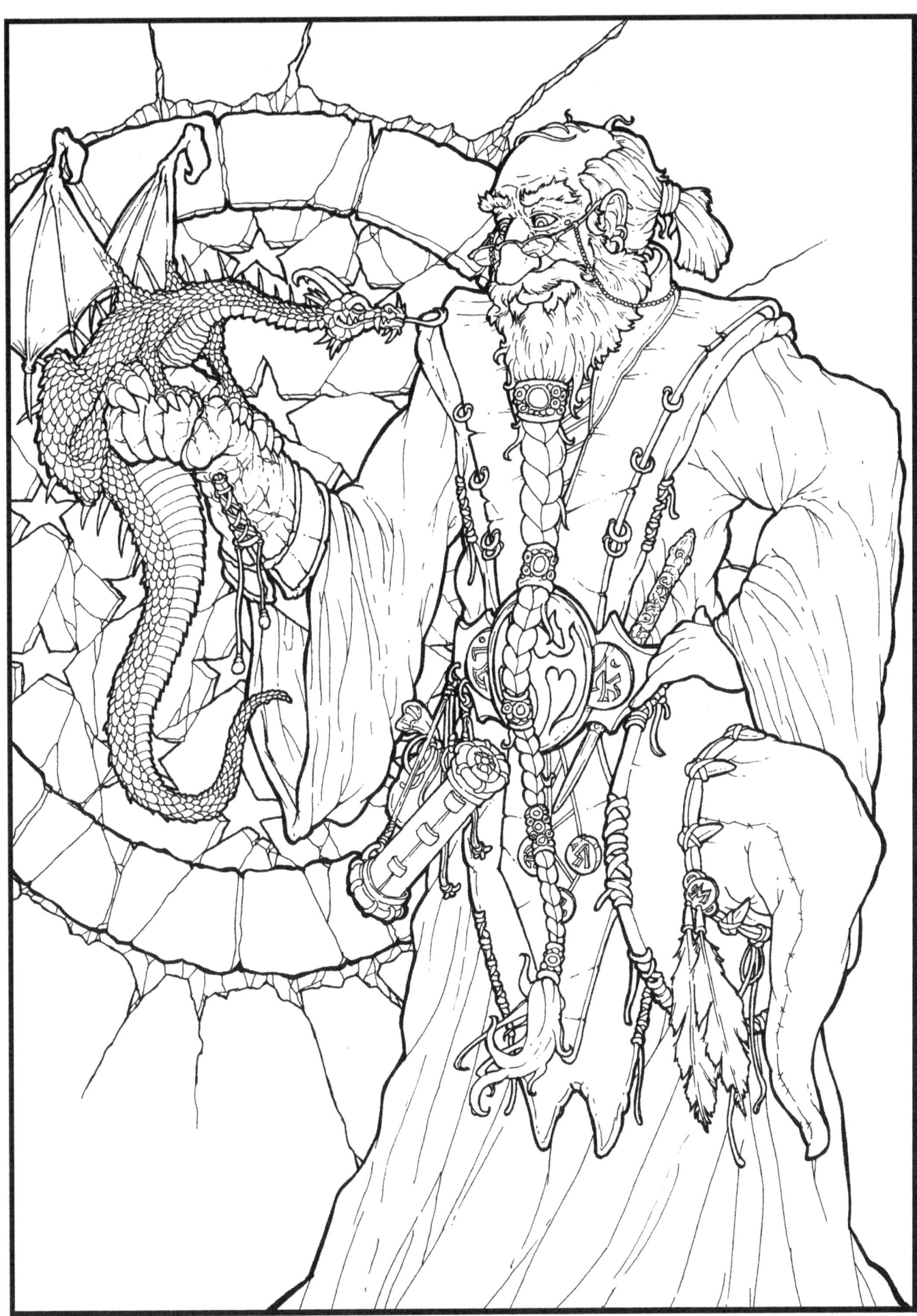

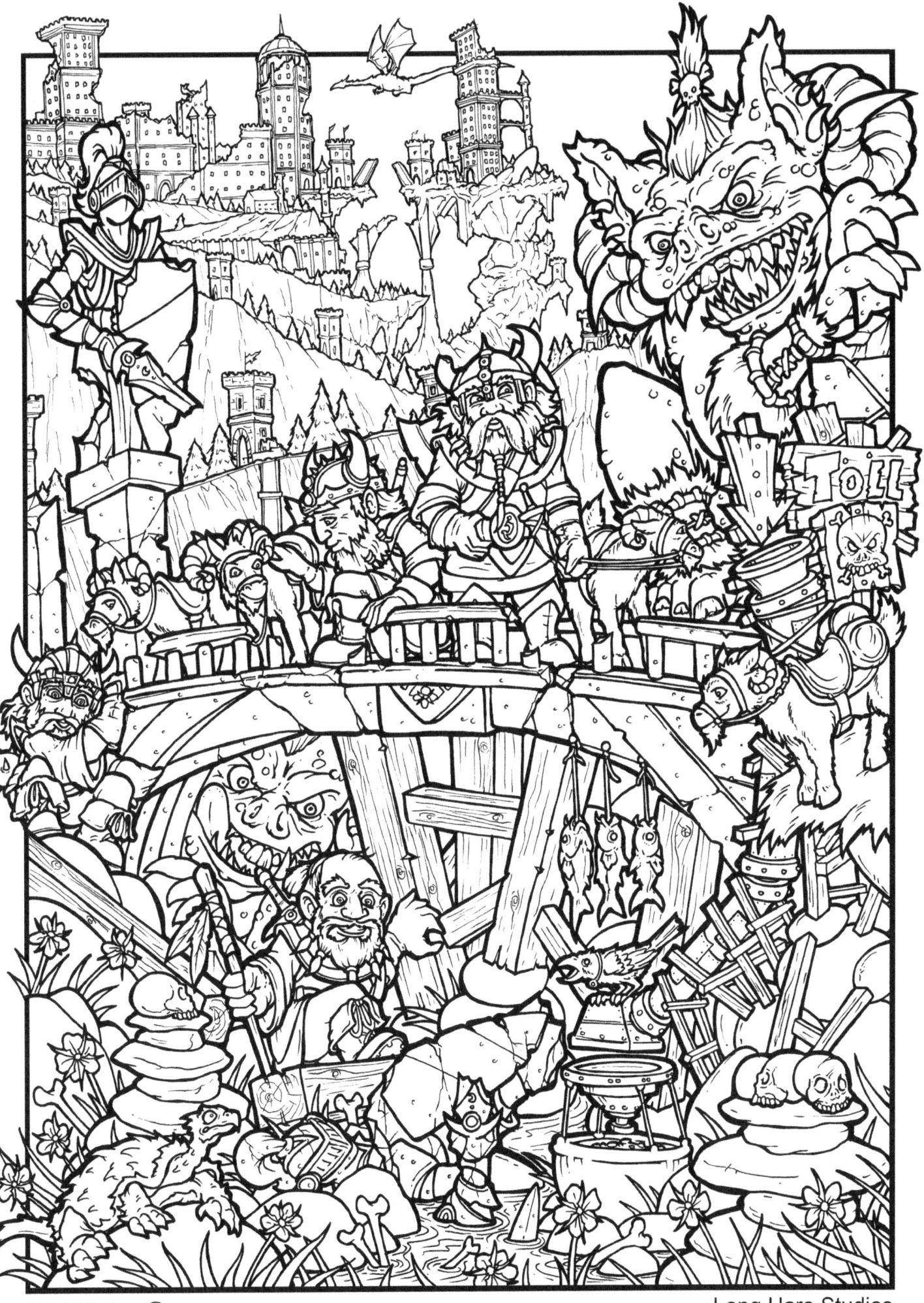

Chet Minton ©

Long Hare Studios

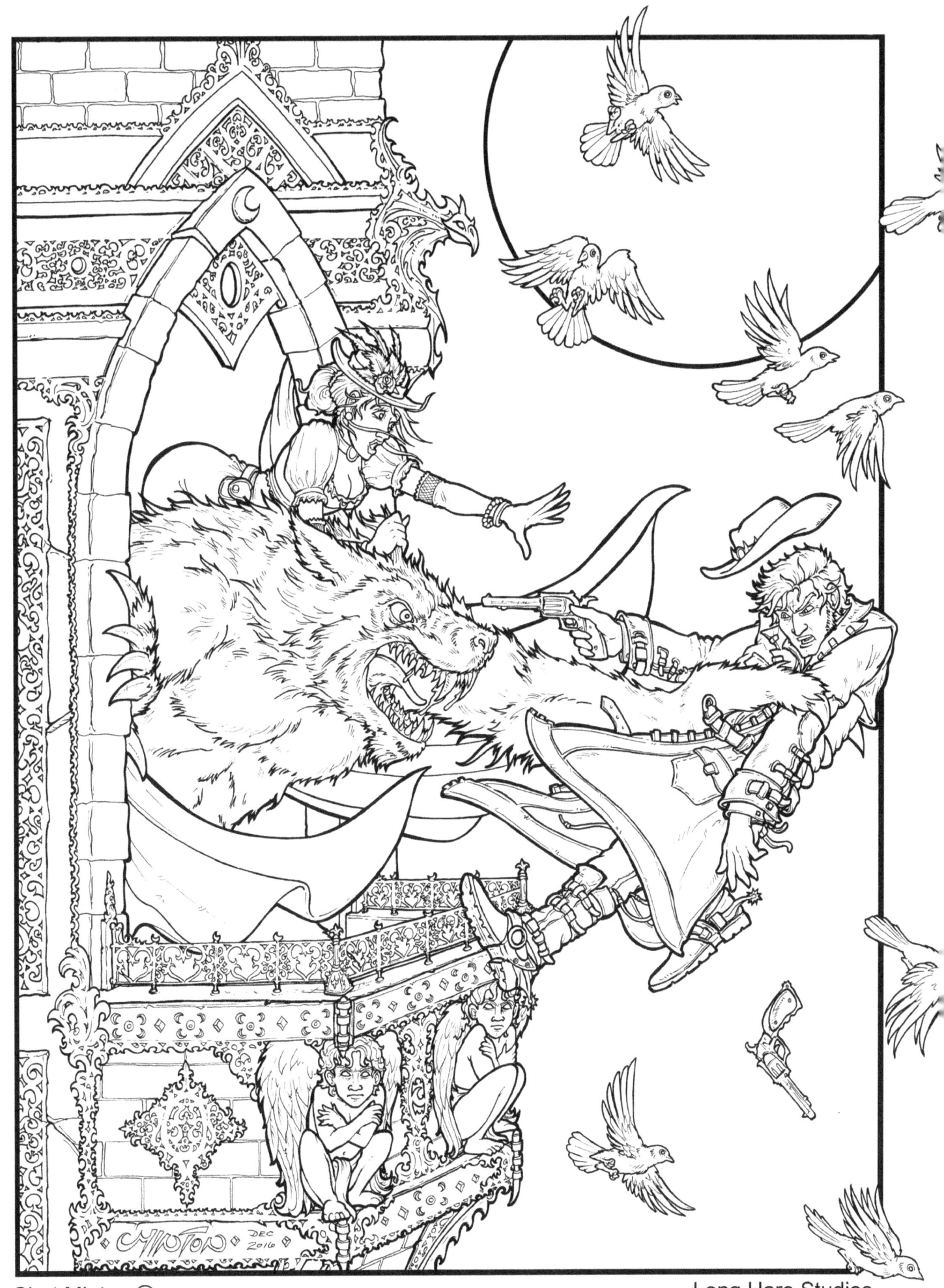

Chet Minton ©

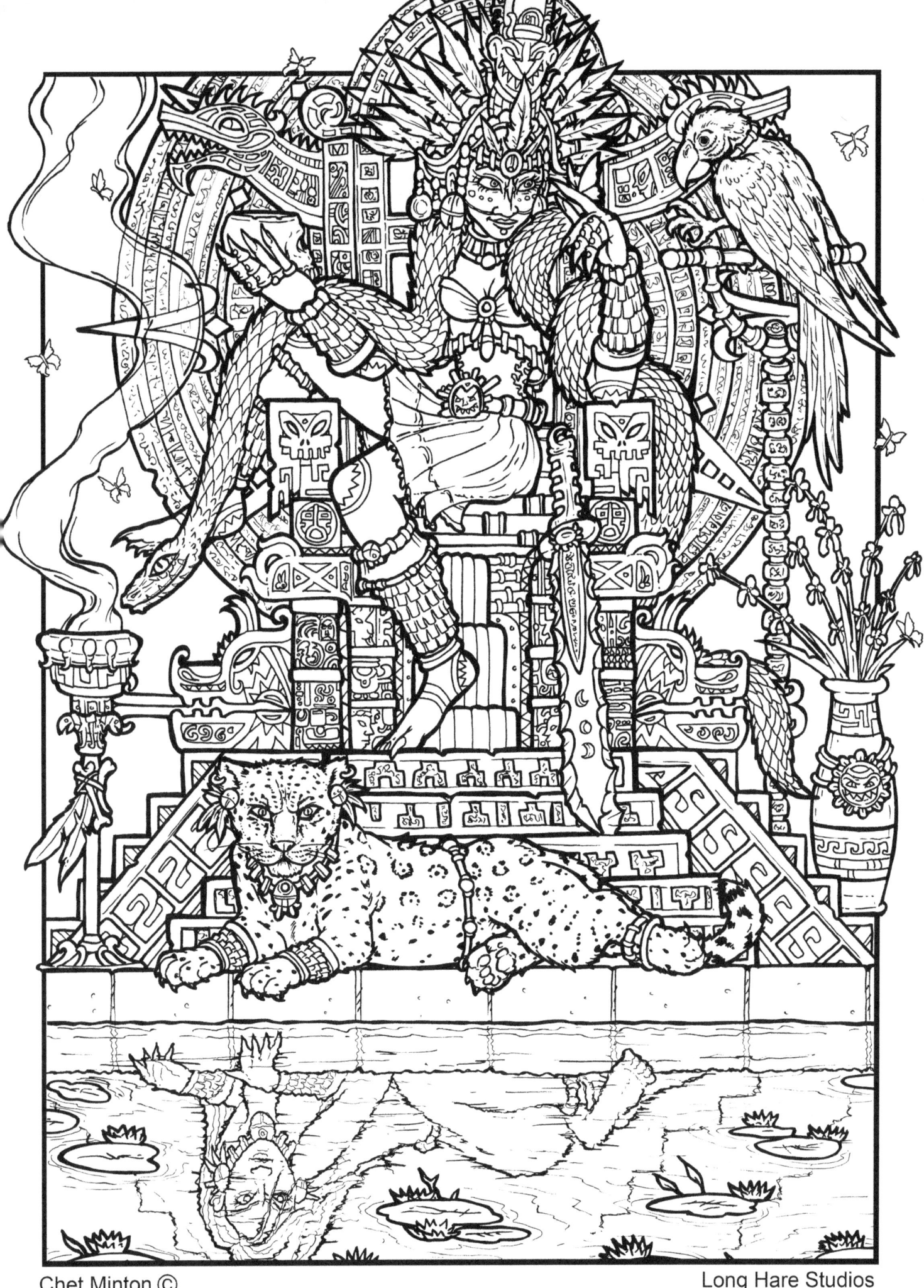

Chet Minton ©

Long Hare Studios

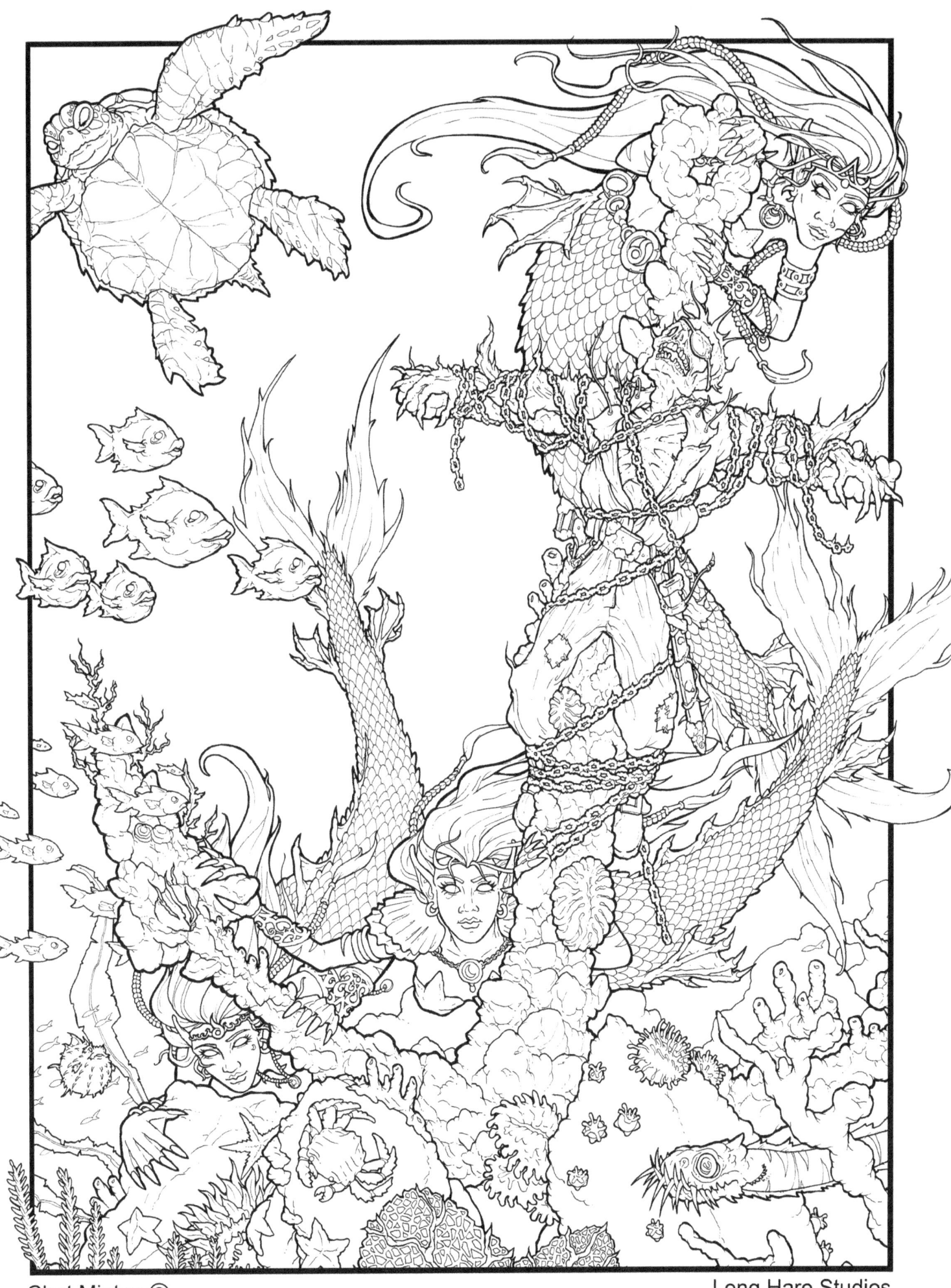

Chet Minton ©

Long Hare Studios

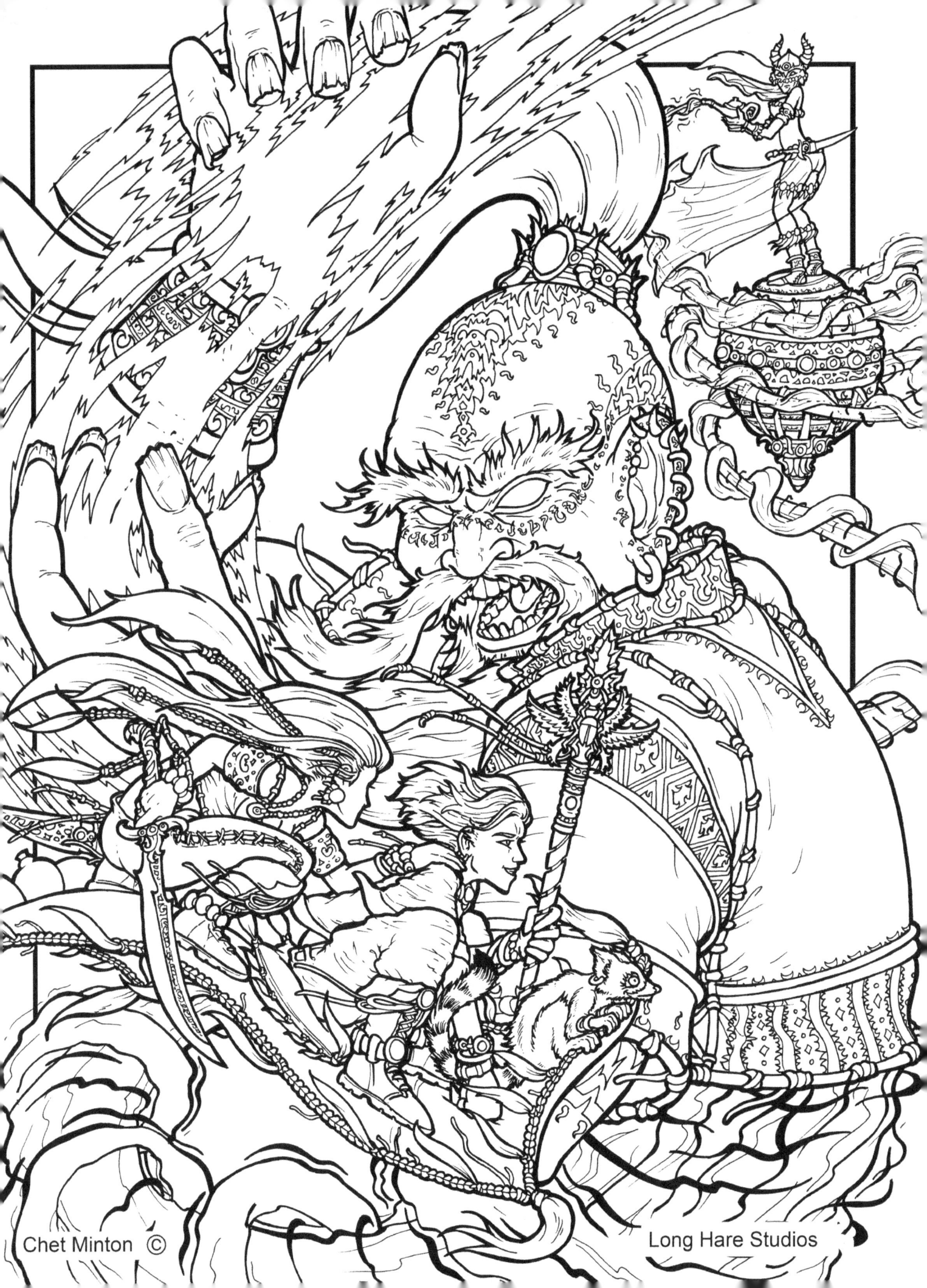

Chet Minton ©

Long Hare Studios

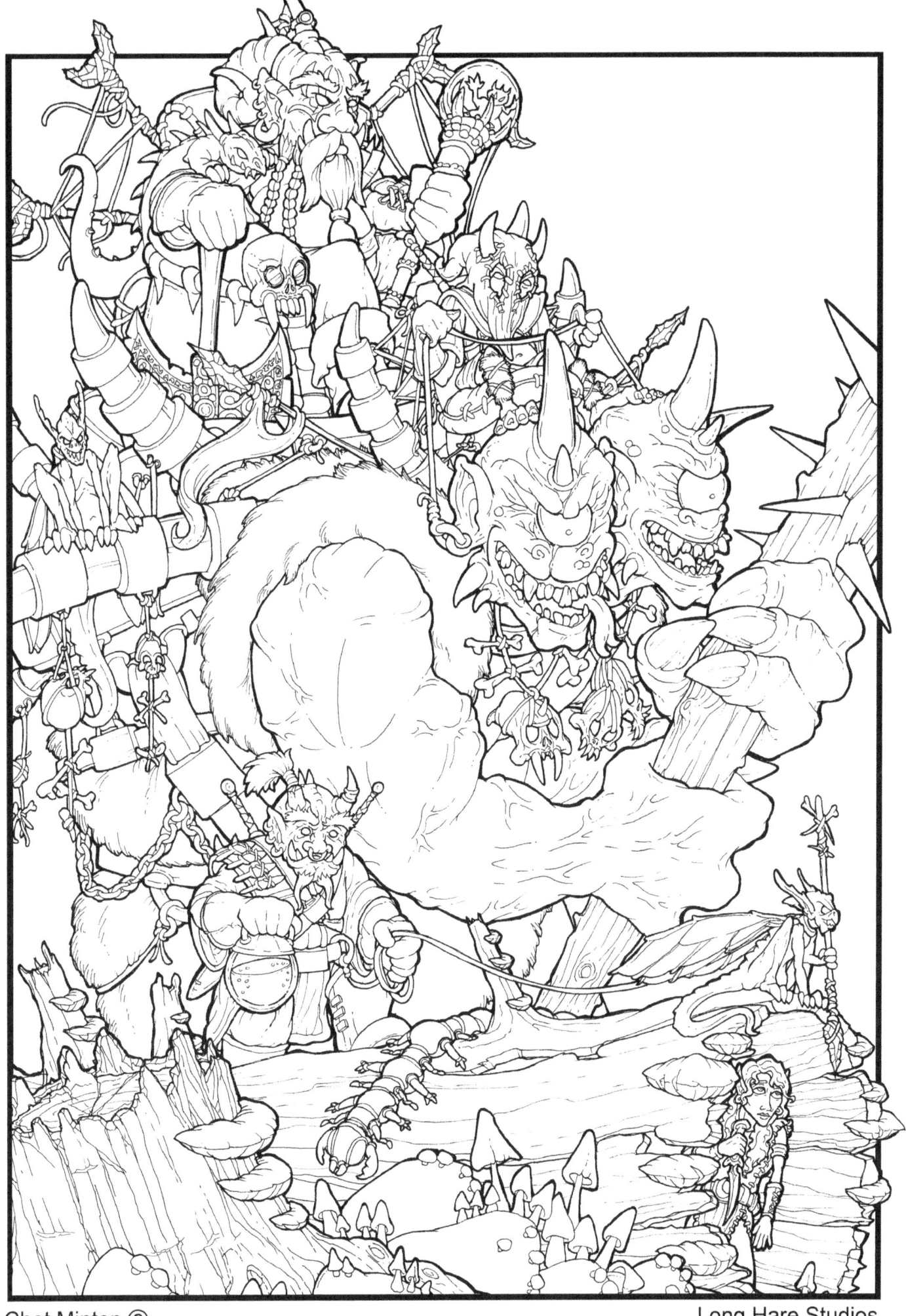

Chet Minton ©

Long Hare Studios

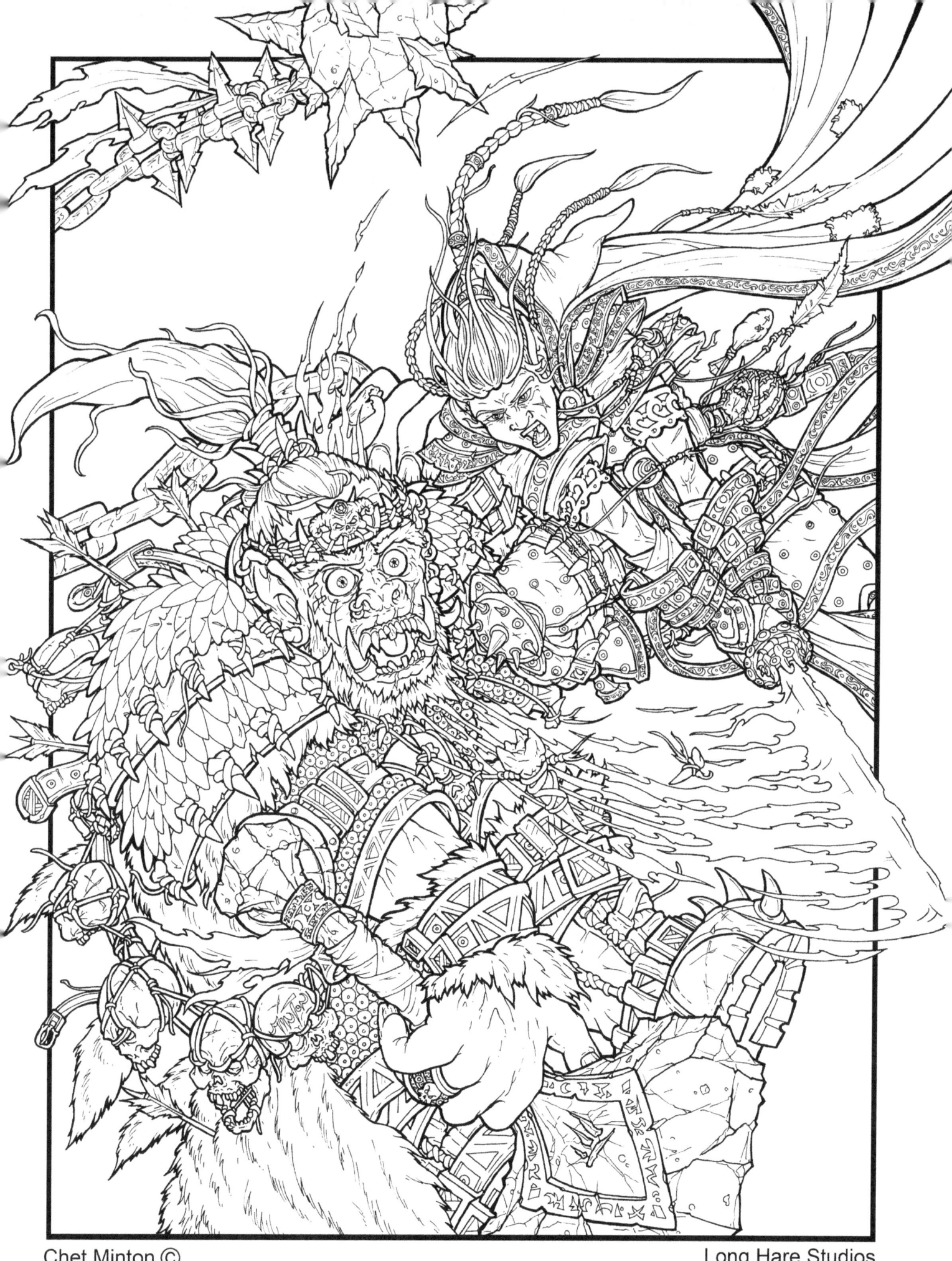

Chet Minton ©

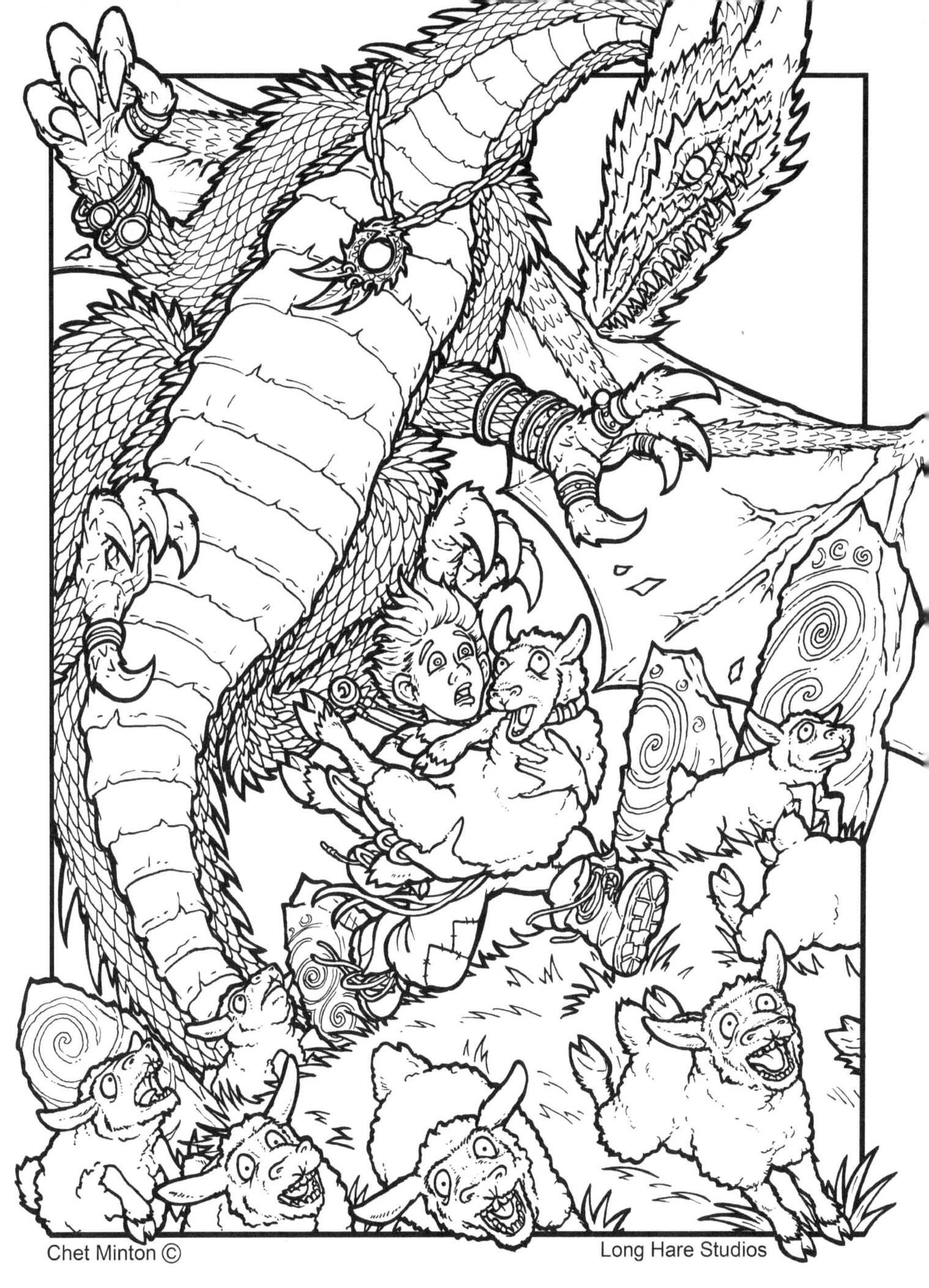

Chet Minton ©

Long Hare Studios

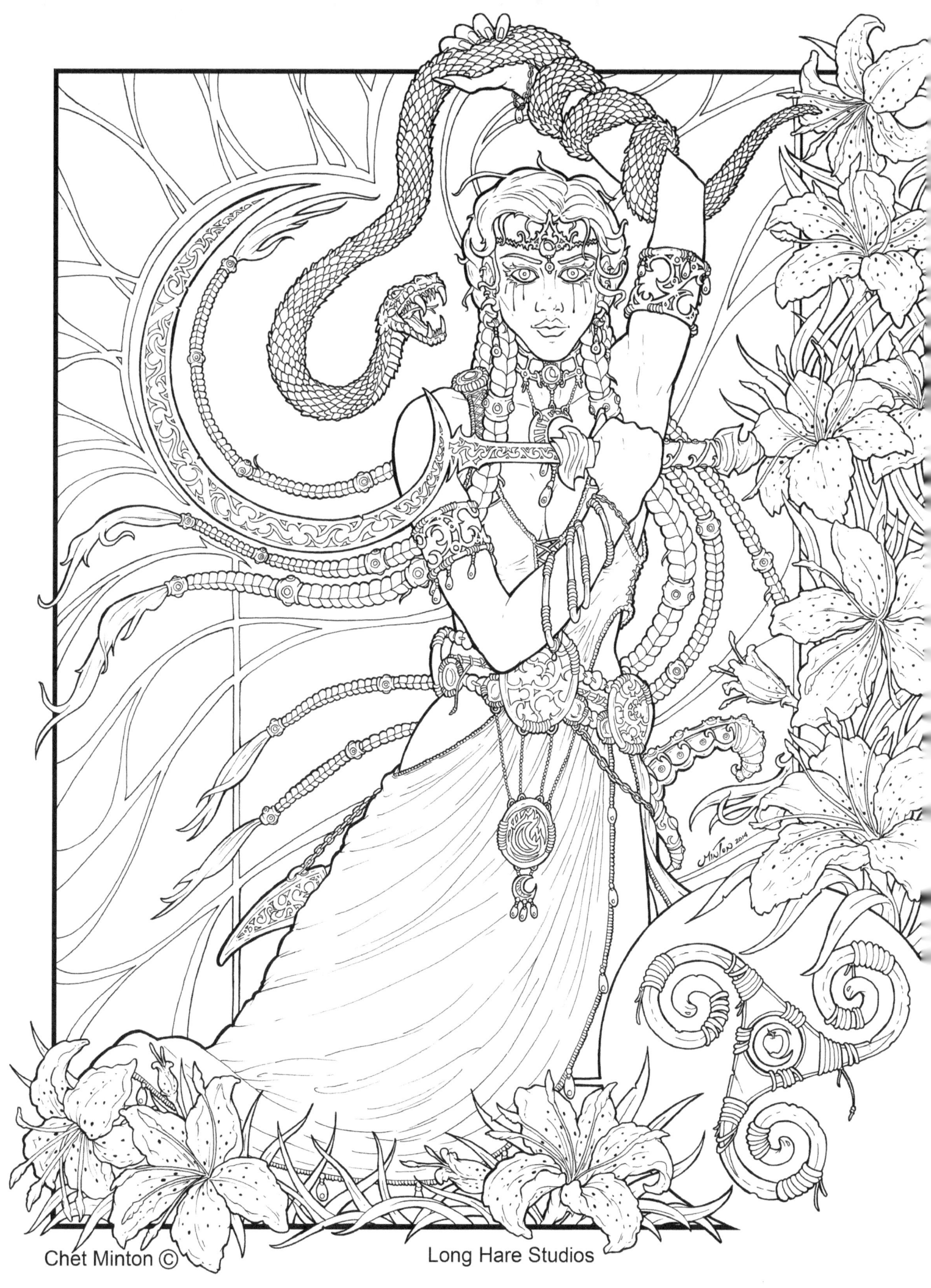

Chet Minton ©   Long Hare Studios

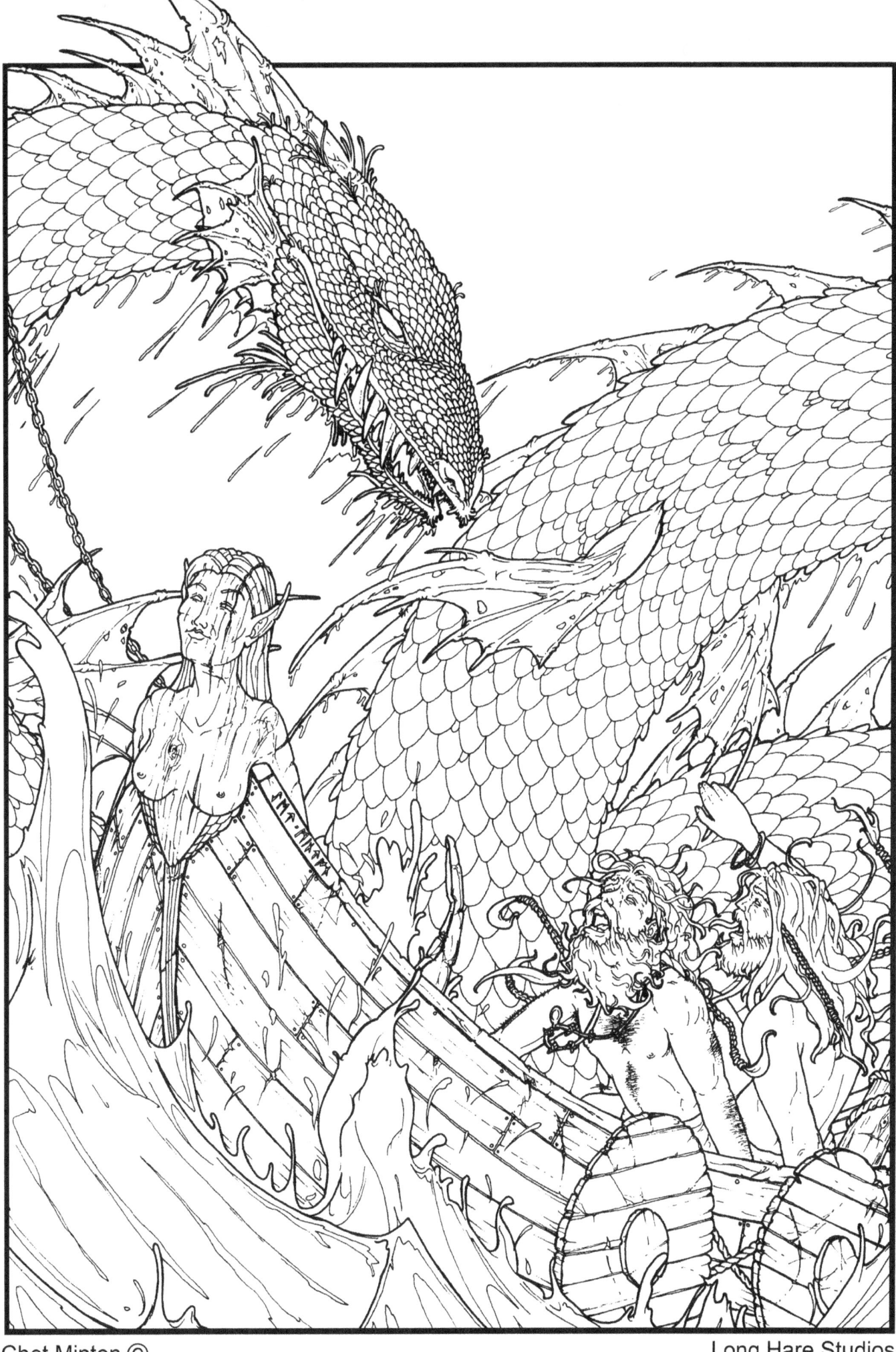

Chet Minton ©

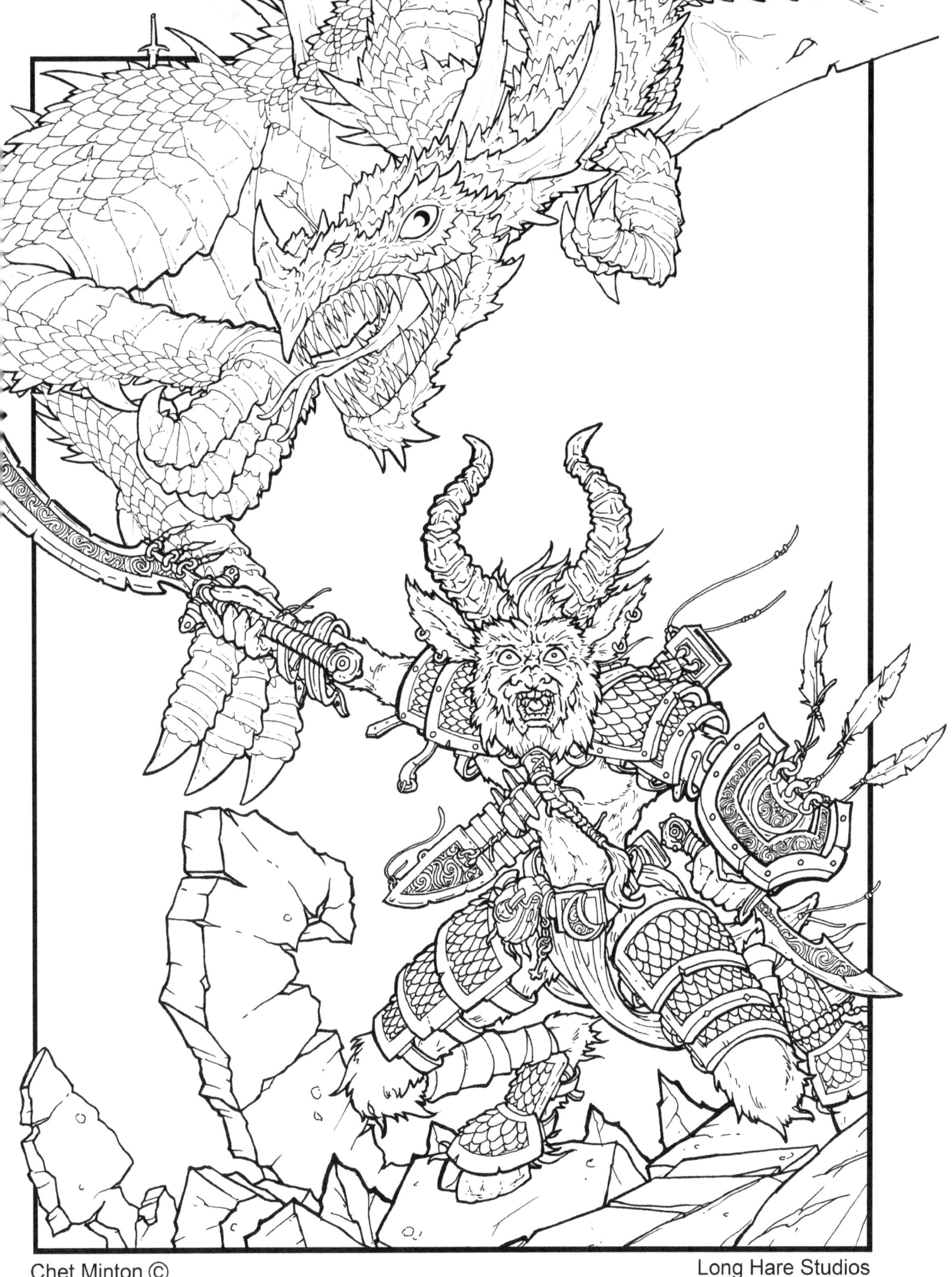

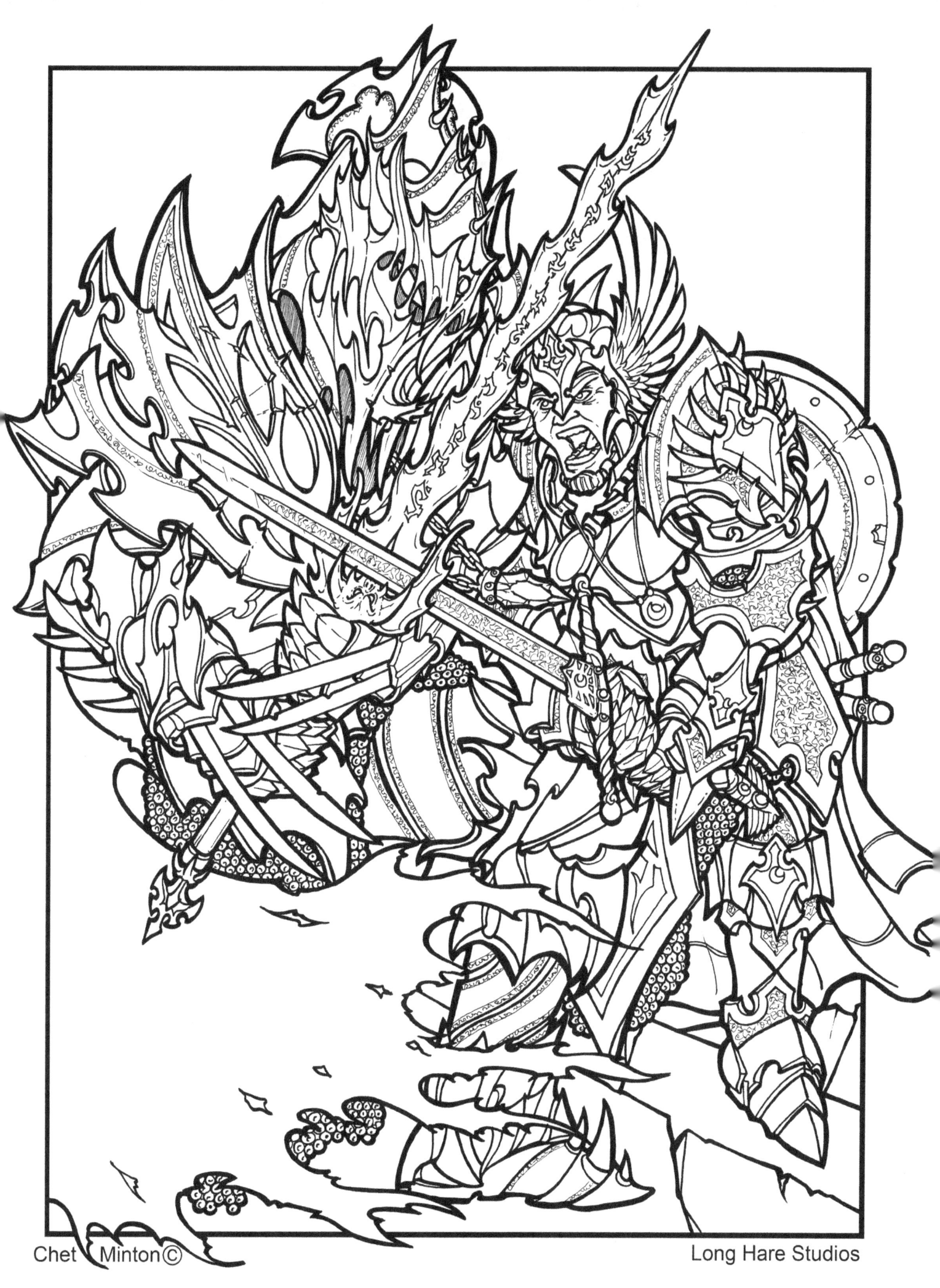

Chet Minton©

Long Hare Studios

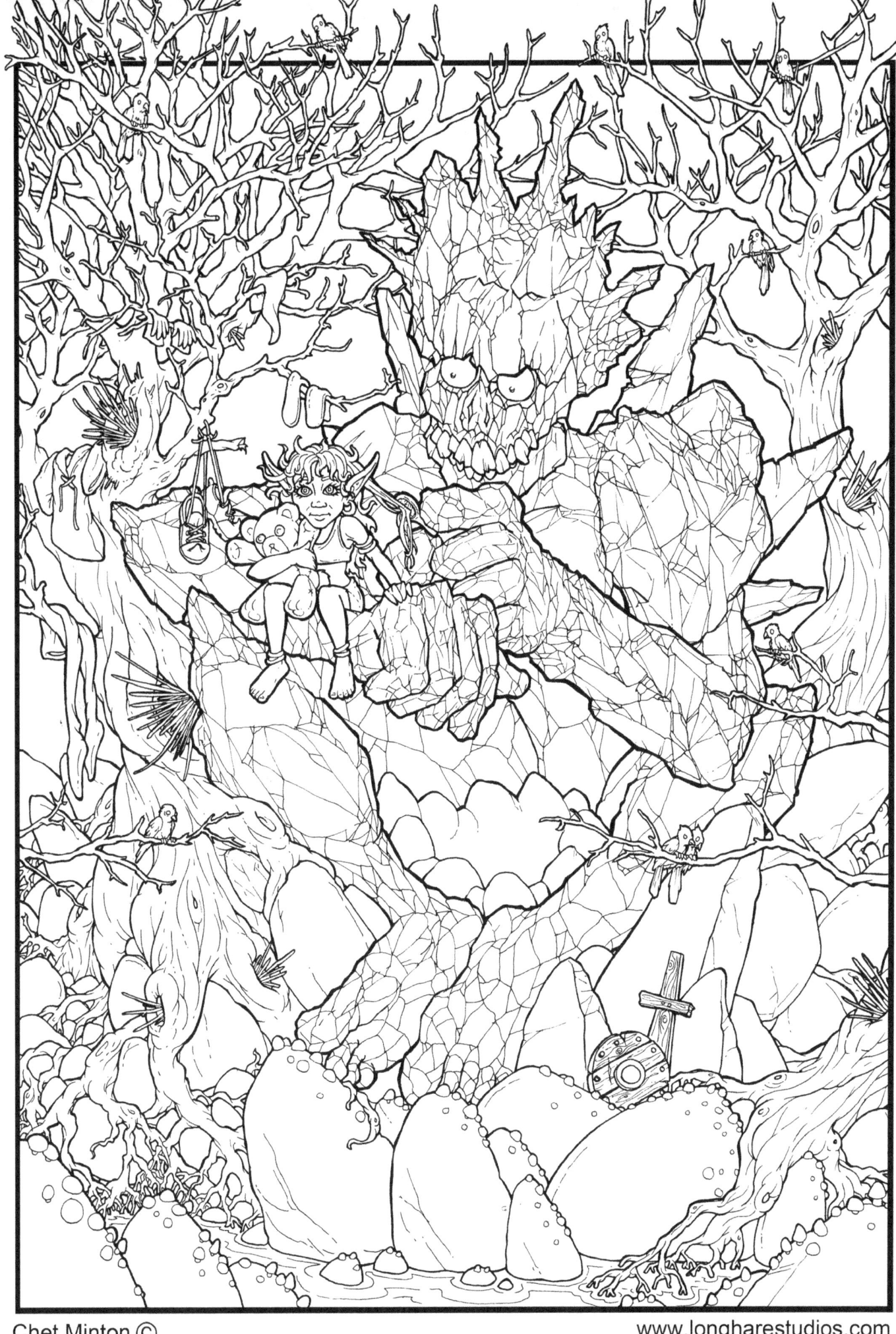

Chet Minton ©

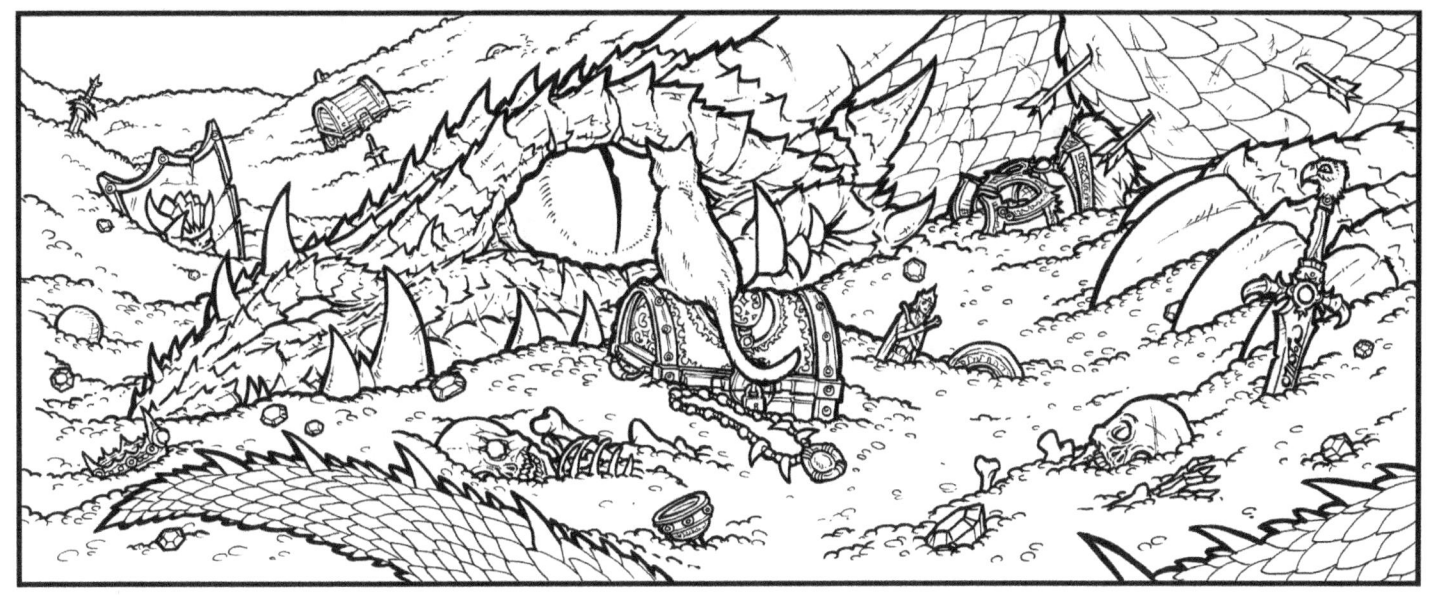

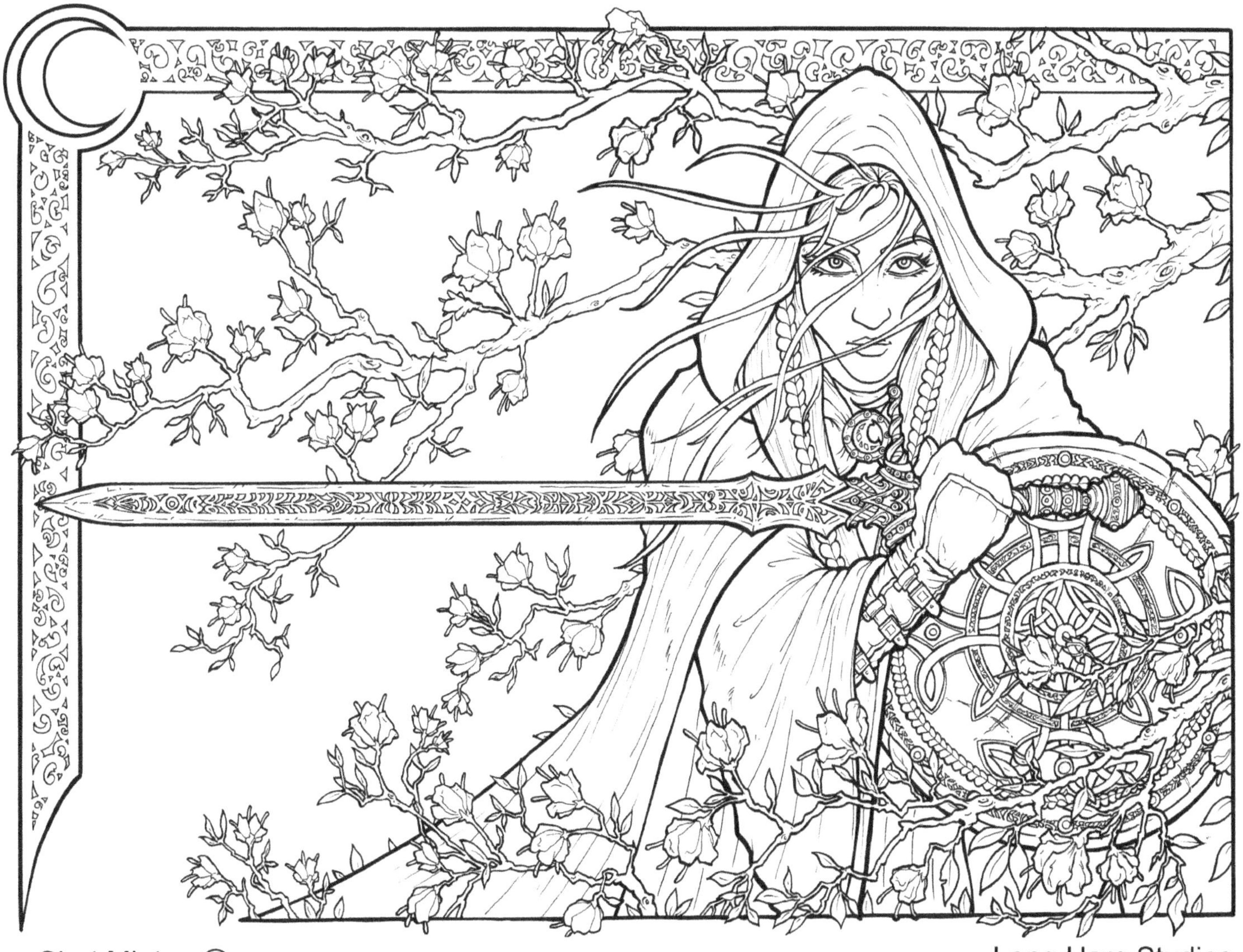